Janet Rees

Fizz Buzz 2

101 spoken maths games

LDA

Permission to photocopy

This book contains resource sheets which may be reproduced by photocopier or other means for use by the purchaser. This permission is granted on the understanding that these copies will be used within the educational establishment of the purchaser. This book and all its contents remain copyright. Copies may be made without reference to the publisher or to the licensing scheme for the making of photocopies operated by the Publishers' Licensing Agency.

Acknowledgements

My thanks go to my family, friends and colleagues who helped me with yet another 101 games. Without their support I would only have reached 87!

The right of Janet Rees to be identified as the author of this work has been asserted by her in accordance with sections 77 and 78 of the Copyright, Designs and Patents Act 1988.

Fizz Buzz 2
MT10772
ISBN-13: 978 1 85503 444 0

© Janet Rees
Illustrations © Baz Rowell
All rights reserved
First published 2008

Printed in the UK for LDA
Abbeygate House, East Road, Cambridge, CB1 1DB, UK

Contents

Understanding Shape

Measuring

Handling Data

Photocopiable Resources

Introduction

Fizz Buzz 2 is a new collection of exciting and challenging games to cover the primary maths curriculum, with emphasis on the skills explored in the Using and Applying Mathematics strand. It is a resource which will engage children, helping them to gain skills that will allow them to understand and describe the maths involved in a game and to develop the confidence to present solutions to puzzles and problems. The focus on number-based games provides a strong foundation of knowledge to build upon. All 101 games develop the key skills of vocabulary, communication and reasoning which further support the child's mathematical understanding.

Flexibility in terms of time, space and resources is a significant strength of this collection of games, allowing them to be used in any part of the lesson or as assessment activities. They can also form part of a bank of homework ideas to enable those at home to play an active part in the child's mathematical understanding and development. To make the games more accessible to those supporting children in their learning they have been set out in strands taken from the Primary Framework for Mathematics.

Throughout the book the emphasis is on promoting discussion and collaboration amongst the children taking part, taking maths from a printed page into the real world. We all learn best when we are relaxed and having fun. Maths is no exception!

Number split

This game for two players allows children to work with numbers to 1000, reinforcing their knowledge and understanding of place value.

Resources

Playing cards: ace (=1) to 9 from a full pack of cards, paper and pencil

How to play

Place the cards face down on a table. Each player takes six cards from the pile and uses them in any order to make two 3-digit numbers. Then each turns over three more cards from the pile. This time the order is fixed: the first is the hundreds number, the second the tens and the third the units.

If the new number falls between the 3-digit numbers they originally made, they score a point. Play continues until one player has a specific number of points, or time runs out.

Comments

Players need to create two numbers with as great a difference as possible between them. For example, 2, 2, 8, 3, 6, 1 could give 122 and 863, with the most opportunity for the final 3-digit number to fall between them. Don't give the players this clue. Let them discuss strategy first; they may find this out for themselves. If not, try 'I wonder if ...'.

Perfect fit

This game is an enjoyable way to practise understanding about inequalities and the notation for 'greater than' and 'less than'.

Resources

One large 1–6 dice, sheet showing enlarged version of diagram provided

$$\square \ \square \ > \ \square \ \square$$

$$\square \ \square \ < \ \square \ \square$$

How to play

Divide the group into teams of no more than four.
A player from each team in turn throws the dice and calls out the number to the whole group. After discussion, each team decides where to write the digit on the resource sheet. Once written, its place cannot be changed. When all the spaces are filled, the team score a point if they have created a true statement. If the statement is untrue, no points are scored.

Comments

Encourage discussion between group members before they decide where to place the digit. This will develop communication and discussion skills, as well as logical thinking. You could change the resource sheet: add an extra box to each side (for 3-digit numbers) or include a decimal point.

Higher or lower?

This game uses children's understanding of place value and ordering. It can be used for looking at properties of numbers as well as providing an opportunity for discussing probabilities.

Resources

0–20 number cards

How to play

Group the children into pairs or teams of no more than four. Shuffle the cards, put them in a pile face down, and turn over the top card. Read out the number. Before turning over the next card, ask pairs/teams to discuss whether they think the number will be higher or lower. Children put their hands up if they think it will be higher, or put them on the ground if they think it will be lower. Show the next card while the children have their hands in position. Each pair/team that has chosen the right answer scores a point. Continue in this way until all the cards have been turned over. The pair/team with the highest total is the winner.

Comments

Encourage children to give reasons for their answers; this will lead to a discussion that could be used to introduce the basic principles of probability. You could change the range of the number cards or use fraction, decimal or even money-value cards. Develop the game further by using the related vocabulary of 'more than' and 'less than'.

Fortunes corner

This game looks at chance and probability.

Resources

None

How to play

Number the corners of the room 1–4. Choose one child as the caller. They close their eyes while the rest of the children go to any corner. When all the children have chosen a corner, the caller calls out a number from 1 to 4. All the children who chose the corner with that number are out and return to their seats. The children who are left choose a corner again and the process is repeated. Play continues until there are four or fewer players left. Each must now choose a different corner from the others. Continue until only one person remains. That child then becomes the caller.

Comments

Instead of numbers, use shape names or the four rules of number. Ask the children for other ideas. Allow time for them to discuss the concept of probability. Does this change which corner they choose?

You could turn this into a team game; the first team with every member out is the winner.

Magic circle

This game for seven players concentrates on sequence and the ability to use reason and logic to discover the best solution to a problem.

Resources

Eight chairs, number cards 1–7, space to play

How to play

Eight chairs are placed in a circle and the players, each with a number card, sit in consecutive order with the empty chair between 1 and 7. The object is to reverse the order of seating, with the empty chair in the same place at the end.

Players may move to an adjoining empty chair or leap across one player to an empty chair. The rest of the group may give instructions to seated players. They could be put into teams; the team that gives the last instruction is the winner.

Comments

Challenge the children with questions such as What if ...

• there are more empty chairs?

• the players can jump over more than one other person?

• the moves have to take place in an anti-clockwise direction?

Allow the children time to discuss other options.

Lucky roll

This game concentrates on the ideas of chance and probability.

Resources

Two 1–6 dice per team or group, paper, pencil

How to play

Before starting each team, or player in small-group play, chooses an unlucky number which is 6 or less. This must be available for other players to see. Each player then takes a turn rolling the dice. On any one turn, players may roll as many times as they like and keep adding to their score. The goal is to reach 100. A player may stop rolling at any time they choose.

If their unlucky number shows up on either dice, they lose their points for that turn; if it shows up on both dice, their points total goes back to zero. When an unlucky number turns up, the dice are passed to the next player and the score is adjusted.

Comments

Make the target score different according to the players. Allow time for the players to discuss their strategy: to go on or stop. Older children should be encouraged to use the vocabulary of probability when discussing their strategy. This game can be played individually, in small teams or in a whole group divided into four teams.

Silent sequence

This game allows children to use what they know in order to work with others to produce the answer to a problem – in silence. It also explores place value.

Resources

Sticky labels

How to play

Children are asked to line themselves up in an order that satisfies a certain rule. It must all be done in silence. No touching (or pushing) of other children is allowed. For example, ask the children to sequence themselves silently according to height. The game may be adapted to fit almost any mathematical theme.

Comments

Give the children labels on which they write information for the others to see, and then ask them to arrange themselves in a specific order. For example, they could write their birth dates and arrange themselves in order from 1 January to 31 December, or write the last six digits of their phone number and arrange themselves in numerical order. Ask the children for other ideas.

Quick draw

This game encourages quick number recognition using place value.

Resources

Playing cards: ace (=1) to 9 from a full pack of cards for each pair.

How to play

Two players sit side by side and share the cards out evenly between them. In turn each player turns over one card. Player 1's card represents tens, and player 2's card units. Once both cards have been placed face up, the first player to call out the number correctly collects both cards.

Play continues until one player has all of the cards. If both players call out the correct number at the same time, the cards are left in place. This pile builds until one player gives a correct answer before the other. That player takes the two cards just turned over plus all of the cards in the pile.

Comments

Play with three players and three cards, building numbers into the hundreds.

This game may become quite noisy, so you may want to limit the number of children who are playing it!

Building

This game requires some preparation time. It involves children talking and discussing mathematical ideas and giving reasons for them, creating an opportunity for them to reinforce their knowledge of place value.

Resources

Single-digit number cards

How to play

The children are given single-digit cards, and rules in order to find the others in their group, satisfying the instructions given. The following are possibilities:

'Find children who can help you make a 4-digit even number that is also a multiple of 8', 'Find children who can help you make a triangular number' and 'Find children who can help you make a number that is more than 349 but less than 682.'

Comments

For younger children keep the rules to 2- or 3-digit numbers. Older children could work with six, seven, or eight digits. Include cards with a decimal point to create more flexibility. Change the numbers to money values so that children can come together to make particular amounts. Encourage children to come up with their own rules.

Choose the spot

This game explores children's understanding of place value. It can also be used as an activity for assessment.

Resources

Four large cards with place-value terms U, T, H and TH; six number cards for each team (these will be 2 – 4-digit numbers depending on the ability of the group and the learning objective)

How to play

Before beginning decide what level of place value to explore. Provide each team with six number cards set at the appropriate level, e.g. six 3-digit cards if you are looking at units, tens and hundreds. Display the corresponding three place-value cards at the front of the class so all teams can see them. A member of each team is chosen to go first. Individual teams in turn are then given their instructions; you may vary these amongst the teams, e.g. one team might be told to find the second digit in their number, another the third. The team members work together and discuss what place-value card is the right one for their team member to stand in front of. Children who stand in the correct place score 2 points for their team. Children are allowed a second attempt, scoring 1 point if they are correct this time. If the second choice is wrong, no points are scored. Continue until every member of the team has had a turn. The team with the most points is the winner.

Comments

Blank cards could be used so that children can write a set of numbers for another team. As the children's knowledge and confidence grows you could develop the game through the addition of a decimal point card and tenths and hundredths place cards.

Luck of the draw

This game uses children's knowledge and understanding of place value and odd and even numbers.

Resources

Single-digit number cards 1–9, a dice, paper and pencil

How to play

This may be played in pairs or as a team. As pairs, each player takes two cards from the pile of digit cards placed face down on the table, and uses them to make a 2-digit number. Player 1 rolls the dice to determine who will win 10 points for the round.

If the dice lands on an odd number, the player who made the lower 2-digit number wins the points. If the dice lands on an even number, the player who made the higher 2-digit number wins.

Players continue making numbers and alternating the throw of the dice. The first player to accumulate 100 points is the winner.

Comments

Use the digit cards to make fractions, placing one above the other; change the rule so that odd numbers on the dice mean the smaller fraction wins the points, even numbers the larger fraction wins the points.

Pot luck

This game uses chance and probability.

Resources

Two dice and a pot per team, two counters for each player

How to play

In turn, the players throw the dice once. If two 1s are thrown, both of that player's counters are put in the pot. On a throw of a 6, a counter and the dice are passed to the player on the left. On a throw of two 6s, the dice and both counters (or one if that is all the player has) are passed to the left. The dice pass clockwise around the players until there is only one counter left outside the pot. A player without a counter cannot throw the dice but passes them on.

The player with the last counter makes three consecutive throws. If a 6 is thrown, the counter and the dice pass to the player on the left, who throws three times. The first player to throw three times without a 6 wins the game and the contents of the pot.

Comments

Every player has a chance of winning up to the last moment. Discuss the game, encouraging the children to use the vocabulary of chance and probability.

Bring in the movers

This team game helps children explore pattern and sequence by trying alternative approaches to overcome problems.

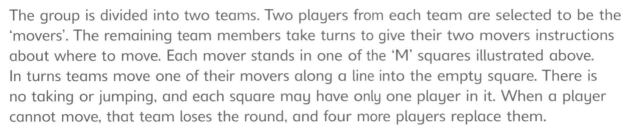

Resources

Mark the area of play with chalk or masking tape

How to play

The group is divided into two teams. Two players from each team are selected to be the 'movers'. The remaining team members take turns to give their two movers instructions about where to move. Each mover stands in one of the 'M' squares illustrated above. In turns teams move one of their movers along a line into the empty square. There is no taking or jumping, and each square may have only one player in it. When a player cannot move, that team loses the round, and four more players replace them.

Comments

The group may be divided into four teams so that each team plays all the other teams. You could set up a league table in order to find the overall winning team.

Number shuffle

This game gives opportunities for children to consider properties of numbers and place value, while comparing and ordering numbers.

Resources

Large number cards 0–9

How to play

Divide the children into teams of no more than six. Two children from each team stand in front of the whole group, each holding a digit card. The children work as pairs to solve problems such as 'Make the lowest 2-digit number you can', 'Make an odd number', 'Make a multiple of 4', and so on. Whenever a pair successfully arrange their cards, they score a point. At the end of a set number of problems, each pair take their point total back to the team. Choose another pair from each team, then shuffle the cards and repeat the activity. When every pair has had a turn, each team totals their accumulated scores. The winner is the team with the most points. There may need to be a tie breaker.

Comments

Do the same game with teams of three children and ask them to make 3-digit numbers.

Add a card with a decimal point for decimal numbers.

Fraction line

This game using dominoes gives practice in recognising simple equivalent fractions.

Resources

Full set of double-six dominoes for each pair

Fraction line made with string or tape, with 0 marked at one end and 1 at the other

How to play

This game is played in teams of two or pairs against pairs. Children take out all of the dominoes with a blank from their set, and put the doubles to one side. The remaining dominoes are placed face down on the table. Players take turns to pick up a domino and arrange it vertically with the smaller number on the top. This domino is read as a fraction. Players then either write or place the domino on the fraction line. If they place a fraction on the line which is equivalent to one already there, they score a point. The pair with the most points wins.

Comments

As an alternative, children arrange the dominoes with the larger number on top and group all the dominoes with the same denominator. Players then draw their own fraction lines and place their dominoes. The player who can find equivalent fractions scores a point for each. The player with most points wins.

For older children, once the dominoes are placed on the line each player adds the fractions they have placed. The player with the highest total wins.

High card

This game includes identification of 2-digit numbers, comparing and place value.

Resources

Playing cards: ace–9 from a full pack, paper and pencil

How to play

This game for two players may be adapted for two teams. Players divide the playing cards evenly between them. Each player turns over two cards and creates a 2-digit number. The number on the first card represents the number of tens; the number on the second represents the number of units. Both players call out their numbers. The player with the higher number gets all four cards.

Comments

If there is a tie, 'war' is declared. Each player turns over two more cards and adds the second number created to the first number. The player with the larger total gets all of the cards. For example, the total was 43, player 1 would turn over two more cards, e.g. 6 and 2, making 62, which is added to 43 to total 105. Player 2 turns over two more cards, 1 and 9, giving 19. Added to the original 43, this totals 62. Player 1 has the larger total and takes all of the cards.

Play continues until one player has collected all of the cards.

Rolling score

This game develops children's understanding of place value.

Resources

A dice and a 4 x 2 grid with a darker vertical line down the middle for each group

How to play

The children are given a target number, e.g. 100. Put the children in groups of no more than six. Group members take turns to roll the dice and write the number showing in one of the boxes on their grid. Encourage the group to discuss the placing of each digit as once it's written it cannot be moved. The dice needs to be rolled eight times so that a digit is written in each box. Each pair of 2-digit numbers is then added, the totals are written below and added together. The group nearest the target number scores a point.

Comments

Change the target number. You could change the rule from closest to the target number to furthest away. Change the score sheet to 6 x 2 for 3-digit numbers – use three dice.

Thirty-six

This game uses the element of chance and probability.

Resources

A dice per team, a set of ten counters per team member

How to play

Any number of players may take part, but it will be easier for organisation to have no more than six. Each player chooses any amount of counters to put into the centre of the table, and throws the dice to establish the order of play. The lowest score starts and the highest plays last.

Each player in turns throws the dice, adding each number thrown to their previous score, the object being to reach 36 or get as close as possible below it. If they go beyond it, they are out of the game. The player with 36, or nearest to it, wins all the counters. If there is a tie, the counters are shared between the winners.

Comments

Because this is a game of chance, the players may be in friendship or mixed-ability groups. The winner will not necessarily be the best mathematician. The last player has an advantage. Encourage the children to use the language of probability and chance.

Word chains

This game may be adapted for all the areas of the maths curriculum and allows children to discuss mathematical ideas and vocabulary.

Resources

None

How to play

Divide the group into mixed-ability teams. Decide upon a mathematical category, e.g. number. In five minutes each team writes down all the number words they know. To begin, the first team call out a number word from their list. The second team then offers a number word beginning with the last letter of the previous word and so on; e.g. count, tens, sequence.

Comments

If a team cannot offer a new word, the preceding team scores a point and starts the next round. The team with the highest number of points wins. For each new round, decide whether words that have been used in a previous round may be used. For younger children this will enable the game to continue for longer. For older children the challenge could be that no previously used word is reused. Refer to the National Numeracy Strategy's *Mathematical Vocabulary* for inspiration.

lucky ladder

This game uses the idea of chance, probability and the four rules of number and may be played with any number of players in mixed-ability groups.

Resources

Two dice

How to play

In the first round each player throws once and tries to score 2 by using any of the four rules of number. If successful, that player scores 2 points; if not, they score nothing. In the second round the target is 3, successful players scoring 3 points and unsuccessful ones nothing.

In all there are eleven rounds in which totals from 2 to 12 are required.

At the end of the eleventh round the player with the highest score wins.

Comments

The maximum possible score is 77 points. Scores of 40 are fairly common.

Each player may need paper and a pencil to keep a running total.

Encourage the children to discuss the scores obtained and, if possible, give reasons for them. Encourage the use of chance and probability vocabulary.

Splat!

This game gives good practice either in spelling the words to be used in their next maths work, or in practising those already used.

Resources

None

How to play

Arrange the children in a line around the room. If space is limited, play may take place with them seated. Call out the first word. The first person in the line calls out the first letter of that word. The second person calls out the second letter and so on. The person who says the last letter in the word then turns to the next in line and says 'SPLAT'. The person who is 'splatted' returns to their seat. If a word is misspelled, the person to say the first wrong letter sits down and the spelling continues. After each 'SPLAT' a new word is called out. Play continues until only one person is standing.

Comments

This may be adapted to play in teams. One person from each team comes to the front to make the line. Play continues as above, but the remaining child scores a point for the team. The winning team is the one with most points when all children have had a turn.

Hit the target

This game is a great way for children to use their knowledge of addition and subtraction.

Resources

Paper and pencils

How to play

Divide the children into teams of no more than four. One child from each team comes to the front, writes a single-digit number for everyone to see and returns to their team. Working together as a team, the children use the digits as they are or make each into tens or hundreds by including as many 0s as they like. They then add or subtract the numbers they have made, trying to get as close to 100 as possible. Play the game again, so that every team member has an opportunity of writing the single digit. The team that has the number closest to the target scores a point.

Comments

To add variety you could change the target number and/or the number of digits available to each team as well as adding a time limit. To help promote further discussion, ask the children to feed back to the group any strategies they used.

Revealing spots

This game encourages children to use their knowledge and understanding of number facts to solve problems and develop questioning skills.

Resources

A set of 1–6 dominoes for each group

How to play

Children work in groups of no more than six. The dominoes are placed on each group's table, face down. One player picks a domino without showing it to the rest. Each player asks one question about the domino; e.g. 'Is the total odd?', 'Are there more than seven spots?' Once the total number of spots for the domino has been discovered, more questions are asked to find the two side values. If neither the total nor the two side values are found, the domino holder scores two points. If only the total is found, the holder scores one point. If the total of the domino and the two sides is found then the holder scores nothing. The member of the group with the most points is the winner.

Comments

Use different sets of dominoes.

To change the focus of the game, the questioner could score points based upon their ability to find the number of spots.

Scoring squares

This game gives children opportunities to use their number-fact knowledge to solve a mathematical puzzle. It introduces strategy and tactical playing.

Resources

A set of double-six dominoes for team play or a set of overhead dominoes for whole-group play.

How to play

Divide the group into teams of no more than six. Put the dominoes face down. Each player chooses four and arranges them in a square in front of them. The rule is that all the sides must total 10. If after making and rearranging the squares the totals are not 10, players may bargain with others in order to swap one or more dominoes. Only one domino may be exchanged at a time. Play until one player has all sides totalling 10.

Comments

Have players working in teams of two to encourage communication.

To add more of a challenge, change the target number or specify squares whose total sides are all even or all odd, or make all of the sides multiples of 3, 4 or 5.

For a simpler version of the game do not introduce a target number. Instead the spots of each side of the square are totalled; the player with the highest total is the winner and scores a point. The first player with 10 points is the winner.

Fast fingers

This game encourages children to use their understanding of number facts.

Resources

None

How to play

Children work in pairs. One collects odd numbers and the other even numbers. On the count of 1, 2, 3, both hold out 1–5 fingers. If the total of fingers is odd, the odd collector scores a point; if it is even, the even collector scores a point. They have five turns. The winner is the player with more points. They swap roles and play another five times.

Comments

Use both hands of both players. Use multiplication or subtraction instead of addition. They could work in groups of three: one collects odd numbers, one even numbers, one multiples of a specified number. Swap roles after five turns; the highest accumulated score wins.

Number sleuth

This game covers knowledge, understanding and reasoning about numbers.

Resources

Number cards

How to play

Each child is given a number card, which they look at and show you so you can make a note of them. They may be limited to whole numbers below 50, or extended to 100 and above. All cards are then placed face down on the table in front of the children. One child is chosen to be the 'detective', who must find the person with a target number card set by you (e.g. 19). The rest of the group fold their arms. The detective, without using the name of the target number, has to find who has it. The children are eliminated by instructions such as 'All whose number, is even, unfold your arms.' Once the puzzle is solved, a new detective is chosen.

Comments

Adapt this game according to ability. To make it slightly more difficult, the detective could question only one child at a time. For example, 'If you double your number, what do you get?' Each child must be asked a different question. This works well with small groups. Change the set of number cards, to include multiples of a number, factors of a number or different money values. To control the length of the game limit the number of questions the detective may ask.

The duel

Several attempts may be required to solve the puzzle. Children will develop their ability to recognise number relationships, and use this skill to create tactics to win the game.

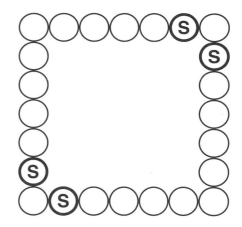

Resources

Game card to match diagram and two counters per player/team, each player/team having their own colour

How to play

Players take opposite corners and place their two counters on the circles marked 'S'. Each player/team takes turns to move one of their counters. Both are active, so they can move which counter they wish. A counter may be moved one, two or three spaces forwards or backwards around the square – the number of moves is up to the player. Two counters may not be put on the same circle, and they may not jump or pass each other. The player/team unable to move loses the game.

Comments

Give the players time to discuss the outcome of the game, giving their reasons for their moves. Allow them to play again in order to test any theories or new tactics.

Either or

This game gives practice in place value, comparing numbers and knowledge and understanding of number facts.

Resources

None

How to play

This game involves the whole group working as teams of no more than six, preferably mixed ability. Say a number. A team member must state that number in a different way – e.g. 24 could be 20 plus 4 or 12 x 2, and so on. Each team must find a different way to express the start number. For each correct statement the team scores a point. Each team has a turn in order, but towards the end some teams may run out of ideas. At this point, other teams may carry on. When all teams have run out of ideas, the start number is changed.

Comments

Change the order of the starting groups. This allows all groups to have one easy start to the game. The game may be limited to addition and subtraction, or include multiplication and division. Use money values instead of numbers, or fractions and decimals.

Pairs

This enjoyable game develops communication, logic and strategy skills.

Resources

Space to play

How to play

Sixteen players stand so that a 4 x 4 grid is formed. The rest of the children are divided into two teams. They take turns to remove two players from the grid. The pair removed must be next to each other. The team which removes the last pair wins the game. Allow time for the teams to discuss their strategy and come to some agreement. Encourage them to give reasons for their choices.

Comments

To extend the game, enlarge the grid to 5 x 5. If necessary, mark the grid on the floor for younger players. If space is a problem you could give players a base sheet with the grid drawn on it, substitute counters for people, and play the game as above.

Twisting tables

This game allows players to rehearse multiplication facts up to 10 x 10. Encourage discussion about how to place each domino to get the highest score.

Resources

A full set of double-six dominoes, scrap paper

How to play

Each group of six players is put into three lots of two players. Players remove the double zero and spread the remaining dominoes face down on the table. Each pair selects eight, decides how to read their dominoes as 2-digit numbers, and arranges as many of the numbers as possible into a times table set. For example, 1–2, 2–4 and 3–0 could belong to the 3 times table.

To score, each pair multiplies the number of dominoes in each set by the set's times table. The total of each set's score is their score for the round.

Example of scoring

1–2, 2–4, 3–0 and 6–6 would give 12, 24, 30 and 66, which all belong in the 6 times table. This would score 6 (for the table) x 4 (number of dominoes) = 24.

Comments

Players arrange their dominoes in table sets and score for the largest set. Their score is the total number of spots in this set. Players could use a double-nine set.

Teams have an extra child as referee, who could use a sand timer to stop play after two minutes, check that all the sets are acceptable, and keep score.

Property vote

This game reinforces children's knowledge of number facts in a fun and interactive way. It will provide you with a quick overview of children's knowledge and understanding.

Resources

A number card for each child (or children write their own number at the beginning)

How to play

Each child has a number card (or has written a number) in front of them. Give instructions such as 'Stand up if your number is odd', 'Do a star jump if your number is even', 'Clap your hands if your number is over ten / in the five times table', and so on.

Comments

This is a game that can take five minutes or the whole lesson. The children could, as a team of no more than six, pick one of the numbers on their table and write as many properties as they can for it. They then choose a second number and do the same. Continue in this way until all their numbers have been discussed. Children could share their ideas with the rest of the group. Points are given for each correct property suggested. This can be part of the lesson or a homework activity.

Linking numbers

This game uses children's knowledge and understanding of properties of numbers.

Resources

None

How to play

This game starts as a whole-group activity but may then be used as team work. Establish the order in which the children will answer. Say a number, e.g. 6. The first child must say another number that has something in common with it, and state the common factor, e.g. 24, because they are both even. The next child says a number that has something in common with the last one (24), e.g. 28, because they are both under 30. Play continues until each child has had a turn.

Comments

As children grow in confidence, encourage them to think of more advanced reasons, such as 'prime', 'multiple of', triangular', and so on.

To make this into a group game, ask children to work in 2s or 3s and work out a pattern of three (or four) numbers. This is presented to the whole group, who have to try to work out the rule for the pattern. The small group who come up with the intended pattern (there may be many others) score a point.

Out of order

This game uses knowledge and understanding of number sequence as well as reasoning and logic.

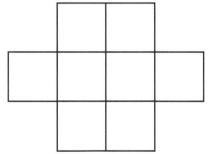

Resources

Eight chairs, number cards 1–8

How to play

Arrange the chairs as shown in the diagram. Give eight children a number card from 1 to 8. This may be done as a team game, or with the whole group contributing.

If it is a team game, one team takes a turn to seat one of their members on a chair. The next team seats the next person and so on until all children are seated.

The eight players now have to be rearranged so that no two consecutive numbers are next to each other either horizontally, vertically or diagonally. Teams take turns to reseat a child. The team that successfully makes the last move is the winner.

Comments

Rearrange the chairs as in the diagram, using cards 1–10.

Alternatively use cards 1–6.

Ask the children for other ideas.

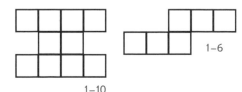

Hot seat

This game covers mental recall as well as understanding of number facts.

Resources

None

How to play

This may be a team or whole-group game. In teams, each team nominates a contestant to represent them. In a whole group, ask for a volunteer contestant. The contestant sits on a chair facing the group. Each team (except the contestant's own) asks them questions that they must answer as quickly as possible. A point is scored for each correct answer. If an answer is not known 'Nominate' can be used, giving the rest of the child's team or the whole group an opportunity to score a point. If they know the answer they put their thumbs up. The hot-seat contestant chooses someone they think knows the answer; they too will score a point if their nominee is correct. The team or child with most points is the winner.

Comments

Instead of one contestant, have a pair or group of children.

This game may be focused on a specific topic – e.g. 7 times table – or you could allow questions on any topic to create a more challenging game.

Move along the line

This game encourages players to develop their reasoning skills and understanding of number facts.

Resources

None

How to play

Divide the children into four groups. Each group nominates a starting player, who stands behind one of their seated group. Ask each of the standing children a question (this can be the same or a different question). If the answer is correct, the player moves to stand behind the next seated person. If the answer is incorrect, the seated child in front may answer. If they are correct, the two players swap places. If both children are wrong, the standing person stays in the same place and waits for the next question.

When the start player gets back to their start position, the next player takes their turn.

Continue until all of the group have had a turn, or play once round.

Comments

Ask questions based on a recent piece of teaching, or some teaching that is going to be taught (as a formative assessment activity).

Get the children to prepare questions (and answers) as a homework or group activity.

Fizz buzz 2

This game helps children to learn and use multiplication and division facts while requiring them to concentrate and think ahead.

Resources

None

How to play

The whole group stands in a circle. You decide the rules of the game. There need to be two in each game. For example, they could be that if a multiple of 5 is said, the child must say 'Fizz' and jump once, and if an odd number is said the child must say 'Buzz' and jump twice. When a multiple of 5 that is also an odd number is said, the child says 'Fizz Buzz', jumps three times, and the direction of play around the circle is reversed. Begin the game at zero and set a time limit or target number to reach. When their confidence has grown, the children may stop saying the number and just say 'Fizz', 'Buzz' or 'Fizz Buzz'.

Comments

Make sure the rules match the ability of the children. You could start with a higher number, say 50, and work backwards using the same rules until you reach zero.

Hidden message

This game uses children's knowledge and understanding of mathematical vocabulary.

Resources

None

How to play

Two children stand in front of the group; they are the 'contestants'. Reveal a hidden word to all the children except the two contestants. The rest of the group then take turns to give no more than 4-word clues that could help the contestants to guess the hidden word. The contestants work individually and take turns to guess. When the word is discovered by one of the contestants, that person stays at the front, the child who gave the final clue takes the place of the other contestant, and play begins again.

Comments

This may be adapted to a team game in which each contestant represents a team. Teams start with 10 points and take turns to give a 2-word clue to their team member. Any clue containing more than two words, or the word itself, loses the team a point. As each word is correctly guessed, a point is scored for that team and the team member who gave the last clue replaces the contestant. Play continues until one team has used all of their contestants. At this point all play stops and the team with the highest number of points is the winner.

Crafty counters

This game uses strategy and logic and is suitable for pairs or small groups of players.

Resources

Counters

How to play

Make a pile of ten counters. Players take it in turns to take one, two or three counters. The last player to take a counter wins. Encourage the children to discuss strategies and ask if they can work out a way to guarantee a win if they go first.

Comments

Change the game so that the last person to take a counter loses. Again encourage discussion about strategy and ask the children to work out a way to win if they go first.

Change the game to use different numbers of counters, specifying the maximum number of counters the children may take.

Collecting cubes

This game involves the children using their knowledge and understanding of multiplication.

Resources

For each team: double-nine set of dominoes, set of number cards 2–10, 12 cubes

How to play

Each team of four spreads their dominoes out face down on the table. One of the team shuffles the number cards and places the top one face down. Each player turns over one of the dominoes.

The team decide which way the dominoes will be read to make a 2-digit number. They then turn over the card. If a player has a domino number that is a multiple of their number, they take a cube. Start play again so that each team has three goes. The team with the most cubes at the end of three rounds is the winner.

Comments

Once a domino has been used, it is removed from the set before the next round.

This will generate discussion about which way to place it, the links to the remaining numbers and the probability of getting the greatest/least chance of scoring a multiple.

Loop the loop

This game allows children to use number facts already known. It can be extended to include communication and reasoning.

Resources

Full set of double-six dominoes for each pair/team, set of number cards 2–12, scrap paper

How to play

Each team or pair places their dominoes on the table face up. Shuffle the number cards and turn the first one over. This is the target number. Each team in turn places a domino in a chain; each pair of touching ends must add up to the target number. For each domino placed, the pair score a point. A team that places their last domino scores an extra 10 points. A team that can place their last domino to make the chain a complete loop scores an extra 20 points.

Give each team a total of 100. At the end of each game, teams subtract the total of spots left from 100. They are eliminated when they get to zero.

Comments

Some numbers cannot be made with a double-six set. Allow time for teams to discuss why not, and to find out which numbers will use most dominoes.

Top table

This is a game for four players or the whole group, using knowledge and understanding of times tables.

Resources

Incomplete set of double-six dominoes, scrap paper

How to play

Players spread the dominoes face down in front of them and take three each. Each places their dominoes in a line and multiplies the three numbers at the top, recording the product. They repeat this with the numbers at the bottom. Each then finds the difference between their two totals. The player with the smallest difference wins the round.

After three rounds, each totals their differences from each round. The player with the smallest difference wins.

Comments

Play the game with the whole group. Children work in pairs or threes, with three dominoes. They discuss the best way to place their set, then call out in turn their 'top' total, which is recorded for all to see. They repeat this with the 'bottoms'. Differences are calculated. The team with the lowest (or highest) difference wins.

Roll your dice right

This game uses children's understanding of addition and subtraction. By working in small groups it allows children to develop their reasoning about numbers.

Resources

A 1–6 dice

How to play

Divide the group into teams of no more than six. The aim is for each team to come as close to a target number as possible. Choose a target number. A member from each team comes to the front and takes a turn to throw the dice and tell their team the number showing. That person then rejoins their team. Each team may decide to use the number as it is, or double it. Encourage discussion between all team members. The team then decide whether to have another roll of the dice. The score is the difference between the result and the target number. Each team has six turns and then the scores are totalled. The winning team is the one with the lowest score.

Comments

Use a different dice. Aim for higher or lower numbers. Choose a low target number (under 10), throw a 1–20 dice and use halving as well as doubling; this will involve decimals. The target number could be a starting point and the teams have to get back to zero.

Dot to dot

This game is ideal for children who are still at the early stages of calculation. It focuses on understanding addition.

Resources

A double-six set of dominoes

How to play

Group the children into teams of four. Spread the dominoes face down on the table. Each player takes five and places them face down in front of them in a line. Place a domino from the leftover pile in the middle of the group, face up. In turn each player turns over one domino at the left end of their line. If it matches either end of the central domino, they join it to the domino. If it doesn't match, they place it face up at the right end of their line. On their next turn they use the new left domino.

The first player to match all dominoes wins. If all dominoes have been turned over and none matches the central play, the game ends. The player with the lowest total of spots on their remaining dominoes wins.

Comments

Play several games. Players keep a running total of the spots left in their line. When a player has a total of twenty or more the game ends and the player with the least number of spots wins. They could play in pairs, with a line of seven dominoes.

Rolling along

This game develops children's confidence to use a variety of calculating operations simultaneously.

Resources

A 0–9 dice, pencils and paper

How to play

Children should be in groups of no more than four. Choose three children to throw the dice once each to give a 3-digit target number. Choose six more to throw the dice once each to give six single-digit numbers. Set a time limit.

Each group/pair may use any of the six single-digit numbers as often as they like, with any of the operations, to make the target number. If a group has found a way, they may go on to find another. Points may be given according to the number of ways, or to the first group to offer a solution.

Comments

Use a 2-digit target number and two or three single-digit numbers. Use a sliding scale for scoring: 5 points for hitting the target down to 1 for four off it.

Find a home

This game encourages recall of addition facts for pairs of numbers.

Resources

A set of double-six dominoes between two pairs, Blu-Tack®

How to play

This game is played in pairs. Demonstrate the game first by asking a child to play with you. Write the numbers from 0 to 12 on the board. Take seven dominoes each from a full set and keep the dominoes you have a secret. Take turns to choose one of your dominoes and calculate the total number of spots. Find that number on the board and stick the domino underneath it if there is a space. If there is already a domino under the number, another may not be placed there.

Continue until neither player has a domino that matches the remaining numbers. The player with the fewest dominoes left wins. If both players have the same number of dominoes left, the player with the smaller total of spots wins.

Comments

Children can play the game in pairs with half a set of dominoes. Split the sets so that the totals are distributed as evenly as possible between the pairs.

To build strategy skills, four children share a set of dominoes and play as two teams using two sheets with the numbers 0 to 12. Each team may place a domino on either sheet. In this version players don't keep their dominoes a secret, which allows them to try to outmanoeuvre each other.

To provide a more challenging game, each pair uses eighteen dominoes from a double-nine set and the numbers 0–18.

Roll to score

This game is for two players or teams. It involves addition or multiplication.

Resources

Two 1–6 dice, paper and pencil

How to play

One player or team is 'odd', the other 'even'. Decide whether to add or multiply the score. The 'even' player or the first member of the team starts, by throwing the two dice and adding or multiplying. If the total is even, they will score that amount, but if the total is odd the player or team score nothing. The 'odd' player (or team) takes their turn. The winner is the player or team with the highest score after ten throws (or when the whole team have had one or two turns each).

Comments

The game may be played with different dice, for instance fraction or decimal. This will make it more challenging for older children.

Beat the difference

This game requires careful use of addition skills.

Resources

A double-six set of dominoes

How to play

This game is for 2–4 players. Players spread the dominoes face down on the table. At the beginning of each round each player picks four dominoes. In turn, players arrange their four dominoes into two pairs. The aim is to get the smallest possible difference between the spot total of each pair. Each player says how many spots are on each of their pairs, and the other players agree the difference between these totals and record it. When every player has had a turn, they return their dominoes to the table, shuffle them and take another four dominoes each. The player with the lowest score after five rounds is the winner.

Comments

This version offers the opportunity for strategic thinking. Children play in groups of three and start with eight dominoes each. In the first round each player chooses two pairs from their eight dominoes and finds and records the difference. They then discard these dominoes. In the second round they repeat this with their remaining dominoes.

Set square

This challenging game helps children develop strong mental addition skills and provides an opportunity to apply logic and reasoning.

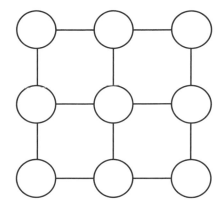

Resources

Nine chairs set out as in the diagram, number cards 1–9 and space to play

How to play

This game is for nine players, who are each given one of the number cards. Arrange the chairs as shown. The children who are not holding a number card take turns to place a player. Once they have been seated, a child may be moved by another player later in the game. The target is that each horizontal and vertical row must add up to 15.

Comments

For younger children, play with five chairs. Each row shown in the diagram must add up to 9. Several games may be played at the same time.

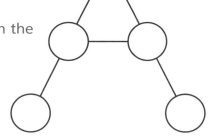

Cross-calculations

This game involves children showing their understanding of addition and subtraction, and helps to develop recall of number facts.

Resources

For each group: two 1–20 dice, paper and pencils

How to play

The children work in groups of four. Each child in the group writes down a number between 0 and 40. Check that each group has four numbers in their written set, then throw the two dice and call out the numbers showing. The children find the total of and the difference between those numbers. Encourage discussion and, for some children, time for them to work on the calculations. Any group who have either or both of the total and the difference on their paper may cross them out. The first group to cross out four numbers is the winner and scores a point. Play again. The winning group is the one with the most points after three rounds.

Comments

Change the numbers on the dice and also the range of numbers. Use three dice and allow multiplication and division.

Magic line

This team game uses and develops understanding of addition and subtraction.

Resources

A 0–9 dice, 0–20 number cards and a 4 x 4 grid for each group or pair

How to play

Group the children into pairs or small groups of no more than four. Roll the 0–9 dice and call out the number. As a group the children discuss and choose where to write that number in their grid. Repeat to fill the grid. Shuffle the number cards, place them face down. Turn the top card over and read it out. The pairs/groups try to make this target number by adding and/or subtracting all the numbers in a single grid line (vertically or horizontally). If they use all the numbers in a line they score 4 points. Points are awarded according to the amount of numbers used from a line on the grid – e.g. if two numbers are used, 2 points are given. Play the game three times. The pair/group with the highest score wins.

Comments

Allow multiplication and division.

Use two packs of number cards and add or subtract the numbers shown to make the target number.

Going for gold

This game is based on a traditional archery target and gives children opportunities to enhance their calculating skills.

Resources

Three 1–6 dice, paper and pencil

How to play

Each team or pair of children draws five concentric circles. The smallest is marked 'gold' and the others from the inside out are 'red', 'blue', black' and 'white'.

Players take turns to throw the dice from the outside of the largest circle towards the centre. A dice overlapping two rings scores the higher of the two overlapping numbers plus the face value on the dice. If a dice lands in gold it scores 9 points, red scores 7, blue 5, black 3 and white 1. Each player has up to twelve turns. The winner is the player with the highest points at the end.

Comments

Change the dice to money, fraction or decimal dice. Use a combination of 1–6 and 7–12 dice.

Hit the spot

This game involves understanding and finding the difference between two numbers.

Resources

A double–nine set of giant dominoes, set of 0–9 number cards between the whole group

How to play

Divide the group into five teams. Give each team two number cards to place face up on their table. Shuffle the giant dominoes and pile them face down. Take a domino, hold it facing the teams and ask the players to find the difference between the numbers of spots at each end. If this difference matches either of a group's number cards, that group may claim the domino. The first group to collect five dominoes is the winner.

Comments

Alternatively, share the dominoes out between the teams and hold up a 0–9 number card; any team that can find a domino with that difference collects a counter.

Play with the group in six teams and give out 1–18 number cards or ask children to add the domino numbers instead of finding the difference.

Counting stars

This game of strategy calls upon the players' ability to complete simple mental calculations.

Resources

Counter for each pair of players, game board to match diagram

How to play

The first player places their counter on one of the circles and says that number. The second player moves the counter along a straight line to another circle, adds that number to the first player's number and says what the total is. The first player then moves the counter along a straight line to another circle and adds on that number. Continue in this way, the players keeping the total between them. The player who reaches the total of 17 is the winner. If a player goes over 17, they lose.

Comments

You could change the total number. To practise a different operation, the players could start with a total number and use subtraction to get back to zero; if a player goes below zero they use addition to get back to zero.

Martinetti

This game uses the idea of chance and probability, and gives children the opportunity to practise mental calculation.

Resources

Three dice for each team, a counter for each player, base board as shown

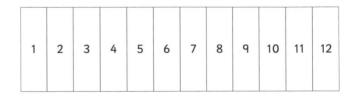

1	2	3	4	5	6	7	8	9	10	11	12

How to play

Each player throws the three dice. The highest scorer starts; lowest plays last. The dice are thrown again.

If player 1 throws a 1, they place their counter on space 1. If they throw 1, 2 on one throw they move to space 2. Throwing 1, 2, 3 would move the counter to space 3. Numbers may be added together – e.g. 2, 3 and 6 may make 5, 8, 9 or 11.

Each player continues while using numbers thrown. When they fail to use any part of a throw the dice pass to the player on the left.

If a player misses a number they could have used, any player may use it by claiming it when the player passes the dice on, before they are rolled again. The first player to travel from 1 to 12 and back wins.

Comments

Limit the number in a team to no more than four.

Total match

This game gives practice in knowledge of number facts as well as using all operations.

Resources

Number cards, either single or double digit

How to play

Children work in groups of no more than six. Place the number cards face down, turn two over, and show them to the children. The two numbers are added together to find the total. Each group must then find as many different calculations as they can, within a specific time limit, that have the same answer as the total. Each group scores a point for every different correct answer given. Repeat the game with two different cards. The winning group is the one with most points.

Comments

This game may be easily differentiated within the class by using single-digit number cards for the less confident groups. The game may also be used to explore other topics by using fractions, decimals or money values as number cards.

Last man standing

This quick and fun game practises basic calculating skills.

Resources:

Five 1–6 dice, paper and pencil to keep score for each group

How to play

Any number of players may take part in this game. Each group needs to draw a grid: in the vertical columns they write the numbers 1, 2, 3, 4, 5 to represent the number of rounds to be played. In the horizontal row they write the players' names.

The first player throws all five dice and removes any dice that shows a 1 or a 6. The remaining dice are totalled and the score is recorded. The same player rolls again, eliminates dice showing 1 or 6, totals the remaining dice and records the score. Play continues until either all of the dice have been removed or five rounds have been played. They then total their score and play moves to the next player. The winner will have the highest aggregate over the five rounds.

Example

Player 1

- First throw: 12446. Both the 1 and 6 are removed. The total is 10.
- Second throw: 233. Score is 8.
- Third throw: 114. Both 1s are removed. The score is 4.
- Fourth throw: 5. Score is 5.
- Fifth throw: 2. Score is 2.

Total score: 29

Comments

Change the dice that are removed – e.g. take away the 2 and 5; it is important that the total face value of the removed dice is 7. Use more or fewer dice.

The hole

This game combines manual dexterity, luck and calculation.

Resources

A shoe box (or similar) with a hole about 5 cm in diameter in the lid, pencil, paper, five dice, dice cup

How to play

Two players/pairs are in opposition. Player/team 1 throws the dice in turn across the box lid. The aim is to get as many as possible to fall or roll into the hole. After each throw, the player/team scores the total number on the upturned face of the dice on the base. The score is aggregated. The highest score after a specified number of rounds wins.

Comments

Make a large hole in the centre scoring the upturned face of the dice, a small one at one end scoring minus that value, and another at the other end scoring double the value.

An impartial referee may judge a 'no throw' (where the dice cup passes over the box edge). Anyone questioning the decision is disqualified and any score in that throw is disallowed.

Tilt

A game of addition that may include other rules of number.

Resources

Large floor dice

How to play

Children are grouped into mixed-ability teams. If there is a difference in the number of players, some may have another turn.

The first player from team A rolls the dice. The number showing is recorded. That player tilts the dice over and the new number is recorded. This is then tilted for a third number. The three numbers are totalled. Play moves to team B, and continues until the players from all teams have had a turn. After three rounds the teams total their score. The highest scoring team is the winner.

Comments

Change the rules so that the first throw is the start number, the second is subtracted from the first, and the third is added on. This could bring in negative numbers. Any rules may be applied including multiplication and division.

Use a second dice with the four rules of number on it, plus a green face for 'have another go' and a red face for 'turn is disqualified'. This may be thrown after each number dice throw, to determine what function the next number must be.

Match point

This game encourages children to work as part of a mixed-ability team, discussing mathematical ideas and ways to solve puzzles.

Resources

Set of double-nine dominoes, set of 1–20 number cards, set of counters

How to play

Each team's set of dominoes is placed face down on the table in front of them. One player from each team turns over two dominoes. The number cards are shuffled and the top one is turned over. Teams try to make this target number by using the spot numbers on the turned-over dominoes. They may use all or any of their numbers and may add, subtract, multiply or divide. Any team that can make the target number and can explain their calculations to the other teams may take a counter.

After each round, teams replace their dominoes face down and choose another two. The number cards are shuffled and play continues as before.

The winning team is the one that is first to collect nine counters.

Comments

A 1–6 dice may be rolled to find the target number; and addition, subtraction and division only could be used.

Teams pick four dominoes and work out the total number of spots on each. They use these numbers as their four numbers.

Chain reaction

This game for any number of players uses knowledge and understanding of the four rules of number.

Resources

1–6 dice, pencil, paper

How to play

Each player draws a score sheet of a line of alternating squares (six) and circles (five) with an equals sign at the end. Players throw the dice in turn until they have each had six throws. Each player puts their score into the squares in the order that they are rolled.

Each player fills in the circles with a sign from any of the operations. The signs may be used as many times as the player wishes and in any order. The player whose total is nearest to 100 or the highest or the lowest – whatever is decided before the game begins – wins.

Comments

Change the numbers on the dice to suit the abilities of the players, including using fraction or decimal dice. Make the chains longer or shorter.

Picture this

This game involves the children in visualising, describing and reasoning about shapes as well as using positional vocabulary.

Resources

Paper and pencils or white boards and pens

How to play

Describe a picture that only you can see. Start with something quite simple and familiar like a house, bird or face. Ask the children to draw this without showing the original to them. When they have finished, the children may share their pictures with the rest of the group on their table. Allow time for discussion about any differences in their pictures. Repeat the previous instructions while showing the original picture, pointing to specific lines when giving the description that applies. Then as a group the children choose one person to take the role of the teacher on their table and repeat this. Repeat the game as often as time allows, always leaving time for discussion.

Comments

For younger children make the instructions simple and short. After group time, some children may like to try the activity in pairs sitting back to back.

Chair pairs

This game enables children to practise using positional vocabulary as well as logic and reasoning.

Resources

Chairs

How to play

Play in groups of six. Place eight chairs in a row. Leaving two chairs that are not adjacent empty, the players choose where to sit. The group discuss how to move pairs of children so that the finish order from left to right is: empty, empty, boy, girl, boy, girl, boy, girl. Only two players who are sitting next to each other may move at any one time.

Comments

Challenge the children to work with the same rules, but change the position of the two empty chairs. Allow the children to explore other set-ups. For instance, what if the number of chairs is increased by 2 and there are two more players, one boy and one girl? What if there are three empty chairs? What if three people have to move together at the same time?

Robot wars

This game needs a large space and involves position, direction and movement.

Resources

Timer, appropriate pictures

How to play

Place the pictures face up on the floor. These may show anything that the children have an interest in and should be age appropriate. Each group chooses a 'robot' whose job is to collect as many pictures as possible in a given time. The rest of the team take it in turns to give instructions; using directional vocabulary such as *forwards*, *backwards* and *sideways* to move the robot towards the pictures. At the end of a set amount of time, the team count how many pictures they have collected. Play then moves to the next team. The team which collect the most pictures is the winner.

Comments

Give each picture in the set a different value, so that instead of totalling the number of pictures, their value is totalled. The value may be whole numbers, fractions, decimals or even money values. The use of directional vocabulary may be extended to include angles or compass points.

Journey

This game develops the children's understanding of positional and directional vocabulary and reinforces their knowledge of both 2–D and 3–D shapes.

Resources

None

How to play

Ask the children to close their eyes and try to picture what is happening as you tell a story.

I have a can of blue paint which has a hole in it and the paint drips as I walk. I start by walking five paces straight ahead of me, and then stop, turn left a quarter turn and walk another five paces. I stop again, turn left a quarter turn and walk another five paces. Then I stop again, turn left a quarter turn and walk another five paces.

What shape is left on the floor by the paint?

Comments

You can invent journeys to describe other shapes. The children could take turns to describe a shape for their friend/group to imagine. They could physically walk the journey being described and make the shape themselves, and they could draw the path described in the story on paper. This game could be used to explore simple angles by substituting 90 degrees for 'quarter turn', and so on.

Hasami shogi

This game of logic, strategy and skill originated in Japan.

Resources

18 counters or cubes per player, base board as shown

How to play

The game is for two players or two teams. Each player/team has eighteen counters of their own colour. They are placed on the squares of the outer two rows. A counter may be moved any number of unoccupied squares vertically or horizontally. The players try to form a line of five counters of their own colour, excluding the two home rows. The first to do so wins the game.

Comments

Extend the game so that the whole group can see the base board. Divide the group into teams according to the number of children: either one team per colour or two teams per colour. Each team discusses and decides on the next move for their colour. In this way children are involved in dialogue and discussion as well as making decisions.

Mind's eye

This game gives children the opportunity to recognise, name and describe 2-D shapes by using visualisation. It also allows children to use reasoning.

Resources

None

How to play

Ask the children to close their eyes and imagine a square, and then imagine a pair of scissors and cut a corner off the square. What shape is left?

The shape left will depend on where the cut was made. Allow children time to share ideas and discuss any answers that may be different. Ask them to go back to the original square in their head and cut off two corners. What shape is left? Again allow plenty of time for discussion. Continue until all four corners have been cut off.

Comments

Some children may need to do this as a practical activity rather than a visualisation activity. After visualising the shape described, allow all the children to work through the activity with paper and scissors so that they can see the different possibilities. Try this using different starting shapes. Instead of cutting corners, they could cut the shapes in half mentally and discuss the different results.

Knight moves

This game involves the players in decision-making, reasoning and logic.

Resources

None

How to play

Four players are needed for this game. Draw a 3 x 3 grid on the floor. The players stand at the corners. Each player takes a turn to move in order to reach the opposite corner using the knight's move in chess (two squares vertically and one square horizontally, or two squares horizontally and one square vertically). No player is allowed on the same square as another player.

Comments

Make sure that all children know the possibilities involved in a knight's move.

What is the smallest number of moves they can make? Allow children to share moves and strategies.

Invisible path

This game brings in 2-D shape, number and shape patterns. It may involve predicting shapes based upon the children's knowledge of shape classification.

Resources

A ball

How to play

Choose six children to stand in a circle, one of whom holds a ball. The rest of the group are asked to guess what shape the ball will make if it is passed to every child in the ring, one after the other. Each child passes the ball to the child on their left, and the shape made is discussed.

Ask what if the ball were passed to the next but one person to the left. What shape would the path of the ball make? Ask the children what shapes would be made by the path of the ball if two people, then three, then four were missed, and discuss the results.

Comments

This game may be taken back to the tables and patterns using different numbers of people may be explored. What if there were five or seven, or eight or nine, people in the ring and the same rules were followed? What patterns would be made? Are there any repeats? Why?

If you want to create a visible shape before asking the children to use visualisation skills with the ball, you could use a ball of string to create the physical outline of the shape.

Follow the clues

The children work as a group, discussing and sharing their ideas and exploring the properties of 2-D and 3-D shapes.

Resources

Set of flat shapes

How to play

Divide the children into groups of no more than six. Hide the set of shapes, choose one and give one piece of information about it: e.g. it has corners. The children discuss as a group what shapes it could and couldn't be. Encourage them to give reasons for their decisions. If a group identifies the shape correctly after one clue, giving reasons, they score 10 points. If none of the groups can give the correct answer, then offer another clue, and award 8 points to the group that guesses correctly. Continue deducting 2 points after each clue until you reach 0. Play stops after a correct guess, the shape is shown to the children and a new shape is chosen.

Comments

The children may do a similar activity in pairs. Make the game more difficult by using a set of shapes with the same number of sides but different size angles, or use 3-D shapes.

Honeycomb

This game uses reasoning and logic in order to work out a strategy, and encourages players to communicate mathematically.

Resources

Hexagonal grid paper, counters (enough to fill the grid you have provided)

How to play

This game is for two or four players. Players take it in turns to place a counter on any of the hexagons, but a counter cannot be put on a hexagon if any of its sides is shared with another hexagon that already has a counter on it. The last player who is able to place a counter on the board is the winner.

Comments

The hexagon sides need to measure at least 1.5 cm if you use standard circular counters. You could make the grid larger or smaller according to the number of players. For a more active version of the game draw a grid of squares on the floor and use the children as the counters. Put the children into two teams so that each team chooses one of their own to place on the grid. The first team to be unable to place a player loses.

Magic square

This game gives practice in using precise positional vocabulary and may be used to explore making predictions.

Resources

Chairs

How to play

Arrange the children into groups of eight. Remaining children take the role of director. For each group, arrange nine chairs in three rows of three. Eight children sit down, leaving a corner chair empty. The directors are shared amongst the groups and tell the seated children where to move. A child may move only into an empty chair beside, in front of or behind the one they are on. No diagonal moves are allowed. The team that moves its empty space to the one diagonally opposite it in the fewest moves is the winner. Encourage the children to use precise positional vocabulary.

Comments

Set other challenges such as leaving the middle space empty. The aim could be to swap the two children at diagonally opposite corners. Ask children from each group to predict how many moves it will take to complete the challenge; discuss their predictions when the challenge is over and the number of moves is known.

Chains

This game helps children to understand the properties of 2-D and 3-D shapes.

Resources

None

How to play

The children may play sitting on the floor in a circle or at tables. Play as a whole group game or a team activity with a stronger element of competition. Choose an object that all the children can see and name it (e.g. door). If playing as a whole group, the nominated first child names an attribute of the object (has corners) and scores a point for a suitable attribute. If playing with teams, the first team to stand up and give a correct attribute scores the point. The next child must name something visible to all that shares the attribute (window), and the next child chooses an attribute of that (straight sides). Play continues until exhaustion of either attributes or children.

Comments

Team A gives team B the first object. Play continues around the table of team B until all ideas have been exhausted, then team B gives the object to team C, which continues. Team C passes on to the next team until all teams have had a turn. Each attribute contributed by a team member scores a point. The team with the highest points wins.

Dara

This game of strategy and logic for pairs originated in Nigeria.

Resources

12 cubes or counters for each player, 5 x 6 base board grid.

How to play

Each player has twelve playing pieces of their own colour. They are placed in turn in any of the empty cells in the grid until all of the pieces are positioned.

Taking turns, each player moves a piece in any direction except diagonally to the next empty hole. The aim is to form a line of three pieces in consecutive holes, creating a right angle. When a three is formed, the player removes one of their opponent's pieces from the board. The game ends when one player is reduced to two pieces or has pieces trapped and is unable to form a line.

Comments

Success in the second part of the game depends on skilful placing of pieces in the first part. Children will develop strategies using logical thinking after playing the game several times.

Try marking the grid on the floor or playground and using the children as markers, with spare children forming teams to give instructions for the others to move.

Copycat

This game involves the children in making decisions and reasoning about shape. It includes describing shape using accurate mathematical vocabulary.

Resources

Flat shapes or linking cubes

How to play

The children work in pairs and either sit back to back or face each other with a barrier between them. One child makes a simple pattern or picture from flat shapes and describes it for their partner to re-create. They then compare the outcome, discussing any differences. Encourage the children to use precise mathematical vocabulary. The children take it in turns to be the partner who describes their shape.

Comments

This activity may be taken to a higher level by using interlocking cubes in order to make 3-D models. The National Numeracy Strategy's *Mathematical Vocabulary* provides a useful reference point for the progression that children should be showing in their use of vocabulary.

Mystery shape

This game has the children working in pairs to solve shape puzzles by naming and describing flat and solid shapes.

Resources

A collection of flat or solid shapes

How to play

Arrange the children into pairs. One child in each pair will keep their eyes closed while their partner chooses a shape from the collection that has been provided for the entire group. The child in each pair who has their eyes closed is then allowed to handle the chosen shape. They may also say one or two things about it. The shape is then put back amongst the rest of the shapes and the child from each pair that had their eyes closed has to come and find their shape.

Comments

Encourage the children to use precise mathematical vocabulary to describe the shape in their hand. Use shapes that are very different to make it easier, or very similar to make it more difficult. Make this into a team game by asking each child in a group in turn to choose a shape for another in the team to identify. The player who identifies the most shapes correctly is the winner.

Shape sorter

Children use knowledge of the properties of shapes to enable them to sort shapes.

Resources

Pencils and Post-its®

How to play

Divide the children into groups of no more than six. Each draws a regular or irregular closed shape on a Post-it®. Draw a Venn diagram where all can see it, and choose two categories to sort the shapes by: e.g. '5 sides' and 'with a right angle'. Each group in turn places their shapes in the correct place on the diagram. A point is scored for each shape that will not fit either (or both) categories. The group with the largest number of points loses. Repeat the game with different categories to sort by.

Comments

Give each table up to ten plastic shapes and mark the Venn diagram on the floor using tape or rope, instead of drawing the shapes. Call out the two categories chosen: e.g. '3 sides' and 'with one right angle'. Any group whose shape has either or both properties may send one member with the shape to stand in the correct place on the Venn diagram. The team with the last shape loses.

Five field kono

This game using skill and strategy originated in Korea. Developing logical thinking may help players win.

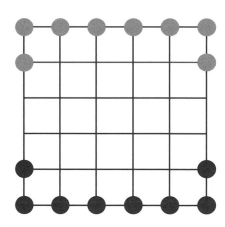

Resources

Base board with 5 x 5 grid, seven playing pieces for each player, each of their own colour

How to play

Players place their pieces as shown. In turn they move their pieces one at a time diagonally across a square to the next point, either forwards or backwards. No jumping over pieces is allowed. The object is to move pieces across the board onto the points occupied by the opponent at the beginning of the game. The first player to do this is the winner.

Comments

Substitute children standing on a marked grid on the floor or playground for the playing pieces. Divide the rest of the group into two teams. Each team has to discuss the move of their player before it takes place. The winning team is the one to get all their players on the opponent's starting points first.

Jumping jack

This game uses reasoning, strategy and communication, and provides an opportunity to use positional vocabulary.

Resources

Chalk or masking tape

How to play

Draw a 3 x 3 grid on the floor. Divide the children into two teams. Place four players from each team so one player stands in each grid square, leaving the top left square empty.

Teams take turns to move one player so that they jump over another player into an empty square. This move may be up, down or across but not diagonal. The player who has been jumped over leaves the game. The last player able to make a jump wins the game.

Comments

You could group the children into smaller teams and set up a league table; all teams play all the others to find an overall winner. Allow the children time to discuss their strategies. Enlarge the grid in stages to up to 6 x 6 to create a more challenging game. Give the children base sheets so that the game may be played by two players at their table, using counters.

Imagine

This game uses children's knowledge and understanding of the vocabulary of shape and measurement as well as visualisation.

Resources

Paper

How to play

Put the children in groups of no more than six. As clues are given, the children discuss them to decide what the object is and then nominate a group member to draw the object on the group's paper at the front of the room.

Begin as follows: 'I am going to describe an everyday object that you could find in school, at home or outside. Try to work out what it is.'

For example, if the object is a table you would describe it as follows:

Imagine a shallow cuboid standing on 4 thin cylinders. The cuboid is about 1.5 metres long, 1 metre wide and 2 cm deep. The cylinders are about a metre high and 5 cm in diameter.

After several objects, check the drawings and award a point for each correct identification.

Comments

Get the groups of children to work on their own descriptions and allow them to use them as challenges for the whole group.

Place the peg

This game is a simple version of peg solitaire.

Resources

Chairs

How to play

Divide the children into teams of eight. One team sits as shown. The object is to remove players one at a time by jumping or capturing them, as in solitaire, leaving the last player sitting on the chair marked *. No diagonal moves are allowed.
One other team decides on the moves. Repeat with different teams.

*			
5	6	7	8
1	2	3	4

Comments

Play the game in reverse to put all the players back on their chairs.

Ask the children to think of a similar game, perhaps using a different arrangement of chairs.

Colour combat

Thinking ahead is the key to this game. Children reason their way to victory.

Resources

5 x 5 grid, collection of counters of two different colours

How to play

This game may be played by two players or two pairs in opposition. In turn players choose and place one counter in any empty square in the grid. Each player may choose the colour at each turn, but two squares which are next to each other, touching along their edges, may not have counters of the same colour in them. The last player able to place a counter is the winner.

Comments

If the game is played in pairs, allow the children time to discuss the options. Some may play the game as attackers, while others prefer to defend.

For an active version of the game children may wear PE bands of two different colours. The rest of the group may be divided into two teams who take turns to place a player.

More mind's eye

This game uses visualisation of 3-D shapes as well as developing reasoning and vocabulary.

Resources

None

How to play

Ask the children to close their eyes and imagine a cube. Get them to roll the cube over in their mind. What can they see? Now they dip each corner of the cube in the same amount of paint and imagine the painted parts being cut off. What can they see now? Ask them to describe and explain the result to their friend or the group. Allow for discussion between groups. Pose questions to the group, such as 'What if only two corners were dipped in paint?', 'What if three corners were?' Encourage the children to visualise the outcomes and describe the shapes using appropriate vocabulary.

Comments

Start with a different 3-D shape. Ask if this will this work for all 3-D shapes. Can they explain why? Or why not?

Switch

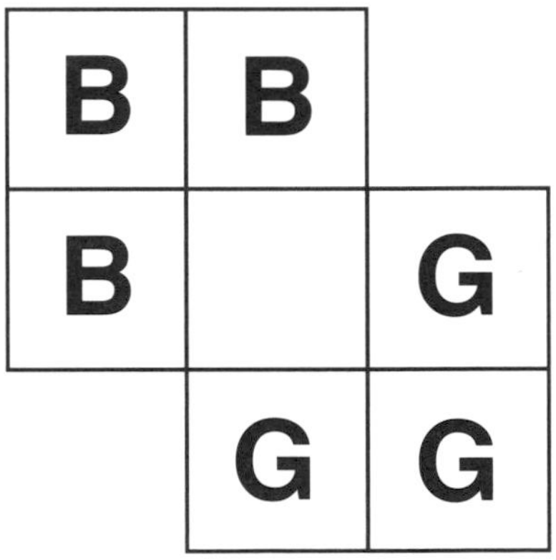

This game of strategy helps children to apply their positional skills to a specific problem.

Resources

Seven chairs

How to play

This game is for six players, three girls and three boys. Begin by setting the chairs out as in the diagram. Players sit on the chairs indicated. Before each turn the team discusses which move to make. The children may move to an empty adjacent chair or jump over one person to an empty chair. No diagonal moves are allowed. When all the players have been moved to the opposite side of the grid, and have therefore swapped their original positions, the game ends.

Comments

Ask the children to discuss what is the smallest number of moves the game can be completed in. Do they think a different layout of chairs would make a difference?

What if a different number of players and chairs were used? Make sure you allow children time to discuss changes to the rules.

Beetle bug

This game may be played by 2–6 players and uses conversions of units of measurement. It takes some initial preparation time.

Resources

Blank dice, set of bug parts for each player (page 63)

How to play

Choose the area of measure that you would like the game to cover. Decide how to mark the dice and body parts appropriate to it.

For instance, you could mark on the dice the following numbers: 25 cm, 50 cm, 75 cm, 100 cm, 150 cm and 500 cm. On a photocopy of the resource sheet, mark the following equivalents on the parts: head – a quarter metre; body – a metre; feelers – three-quarters metre; one set of legs – one and a half metres; other set of legs – half metre; tail – half kilometre.

Players take turns to throw the dice and collect the equivalent bug part. The first player to complete the body is the winner. If a player throws the dice and gains a part of the bug that they already have, play passes to the next player.

Comments

This game may be used for many different areas of maths. Use fraction dice and find the decimal equivalent. Throw fraction dice and find equivalent fractions. Use decimal dice and find equivalent fraction. Use weight or capacity dice and find the equivalent.

What's the weight?

This game practises the skill of estimation and requires knowledge of weight-associated vocabulary.

Resources

Collection of items from the classroom or home, paper, scales or balance

How to play

Ensure that you have discussed units of weight before playing this game. It needs some preparation, which may be done in advance or each player can bring in an item from home. It can be played in small groups or pairs, or by individuals.

Players collect one item each. The items are placed in a central area. Players get into groups, and each member of the group has an opportunity to pick up every item and estimate its weight. They enter this on their own score sheet without other players seeing what they have written.

Each item is then weighed. Group members score points for being the nearest, next nearest and so on. The group with the highest number of points is the winner.

Comments

Allow discussion about the weights and ask them to give an agreed estimate. This is a valuable part of using and developing the language of estimation and weight.

Rock around the clock

This game looks at the measurement of time.

Resources

1–6 dice, large analogue or digital clock face

How to play

This game may be played in small teams around a table or in a whole-group session.

Set the clock hands to 12 o'clock (digital to 12.00). Each team in turn throws the dice and scores as follows (they do not have to move):

- 1 = move on 5 mins.
- 3 = move on 15 mins.
- 5 = move on 30 mins.
- 2 = move on 10 mins.
- 4 = move on 20 mins.
- 6 = miss a go

If playing in small teams, the player who reaches 1 o'clock or is closest to it is the winner. This involves players using the language of time and making decisions about whether it is better not to move or to move. Encourage players to discuss how they made their calculations. If two or more tie, all go on to 2 o'clock and repeat until there is a clear winner.

Comments

Instead of minutes, use seconds and move from o'clock to five minutes past.
Move backwards in time instead of forwards.

Money lotto

This game gives players experience of understanding the value of coins.

Resources

Coin to toss, set of assorted coins (50 in total), 5 x 5 grid

How to play

This game may be played in pairs or teams. Place the coins on the table. These may be any combination of coins, and could follow on from teaching on money values. Each player in turn tosses the coin. If it's heads the player chooses three coins to place on the grid. If it's tails two coins are chosen. (The first player has an initial advantage.) They place the coins on their grid, one to a square. The player with the most money on their grid wins. If playing as a team, the value of all members is counted and the team with the most wins.

Comments

Change the rules slightly. Toss two coins:

- 1 head and 1 tail: pick up three coins.
- 2 tails: take a coin from an opponent's board.
- 2 heads: give one of your coins to an opponent.

Using these rules allows children to use strategy and their knowledge of the value of coins.

How long is a piece of string?

This game involves the children in estimating, measuring and recording.

Resources

String, everyday objects; labels for 'too short', 'too long', 'just right', scissors

How to play

Children work in groups of 4–6. Each group is given an everyday object (e.g. apple) which they must not touch, and each member a length of string. The players estimate the length of string needed to go round the apple and cut their piece. Players use their string to measure the object, and place it by the appropriate label. For each 'just right' the team scores a point.

Comments

Give each table up to six objects each time the game is played. The winning team is the one with most points. Change the points system: for a 'just right' score 5 points, for 'too long' or 'too short' deduct 2 points. You could specify a range either way to count as 'just right', reducing it as children's skill and confidence grow.

Play over a period of a week and discuss whether or not the results change. Do the children get better at estimation? Encourage them to find objects for estimation and recording.

How many?

This game involves shape, space and measures and gives players kinaesthetic experience of weight. It also involves estimation and comparison.

Resources

Lightweight containers, cubes, feathers, biscuits, any other objects; blindfold (optional)

How to play

Children work in pairs; one holds a container in their palm and closes their eyes (or is blindfolded). The other takes some objects of the same kind and puts one or more in the container, saying what the objects are. The first child estimates how many objects there are, using their knowledge of weight. An accurate estimate scores 10 points; a sliding scale could be used to decide additional point allocation. When all the pairs have had a turn, add up the scores. The pair with the highest number wins.

Comments

Use familiar objects before moving to unfamiliar ones. Encourage the children to describe what they are experiencing, using the language of weight and estimation.

Many children may not make accurate estimates at the beginning. The game encourages them to notice and talk about the experience of weight. This game may be played in small teams.

Moving through time

This game involves players using the language of time.

Resources

Large analogue or digital clock, 1–6 dice, counters – one colour per team

How to play

This game may be played in small teams or as a whole group. Set the time to 12 o'clock (or 12.00).

Players or teams take turns to throw the dice and move round the clock as follows:

- 1 = move on 20 mins.
- 3 = move on 40 mins.
- 5 = move on 35 mins.
- 2 = move back 15 mins.
- 4 = move back 10 mins.
- 6 = miss a turn

When a team/player reaches or passes the next hour, they collect a counter. Keep playing until a team/player has three counters. That team or player wins.

Comments

Change the dice used to 1–12 and add more rules.

Change the rules with the 1–6 dice to make more complex time changes: e.g. 17 minutes, 23 minutes. This will use children's knowledge and understanding of addition and subtraction. Use seconds instead of or as well as minutes.

Exchange rate

This game gives children practice in using coins and exchanging coins of equal value.

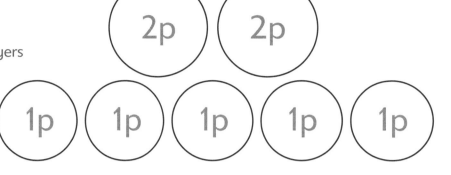

Resources

Game board each as shown in the diagram, dice marked 112233, selection of coins up to 10p (most 1p)

How to play

Each team has two or three players and a banker (who issues 1p coins). In turn players throw the dice. The banker gives them that number of coins. Play continues. Players fill the five 1p spaces, then exchange spares with the banker for the next value. The first player to reach the top is the winner.

Comments

Change the coin values to suit the players. This is a good game for mixed-ability groups.

Find how much

The children identify coins and estimate and check by counting.

Resources

Tins/purses of coins for each team, each with a different value (ideally real coins)

How to play

Play in teams of no more than four. Tip the money from the container on to the table.

Each team decides how much money there is. Children in turn pick up one coin and place it in a face-value group. When the coins have been sorted, they count the money. The team closest to the actual total wins.

Instead of sorting the coins, place together those that total £2 (change the total according to the players); the team that finds the most different ways wins.

Decide before starting if the same coin may be used in more than one total.

Comments

Once the children are familiar with this, set a puzzle for the teams; e.g. I have five coins that total £1.23. How many different ways can that total be made?

Encourage discussion and the use of money and measures vocabulary. The team with most correct ideas wins. Get teams to set a challenge for the others.

Record-keeping

This game gives children practice in constructing a bar-line graph, using the information from a tally chart.

Resources

Book

How to play

Children work in groups of no more than three. Each group is given, or chooses, a book and opens it randomly at any page. They then, in a set amount of time, count how many times each vowel is used either on the whole page or in the first ten lines of the book, and record the information as a tally chart. Using that information, they draw a bar-line graph to show the results. This game requires the children to work as a team, gathering information as quickly and accurately as possible.

The scoring system determines the winning group:

- a = 2 points - e = 4 points - i = 6 points - o = 8 points - u = 10 points

The team with the highest score wins.

Comments

You could use a set book and page number or a pre-written passage to create a fair competition, putting the emphasis on accurate, speedy retrieval and recording of data. The children could go on to use the same section of the book to construct a tally chart and bar-line graph to investigate the frequency of different consonants.

Odds verses evens

This game gives children practice in constructing a block or bar chart.

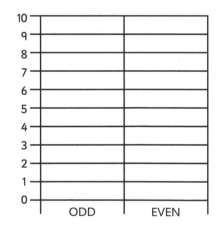

Resources

1–6 dice and red and green felt-tip pens for each pair

How to play

This is a game for two players, using a prepared blank block graph sheet. One player is 'odd' and uses the red pen; the other is 'even' and uses the green pen. Players take turns to throw the dice and the block graph is shaded according to the type of number thrown, starting from the bottom. The game is over when one type of number has all blocks completed, and the player who coloured it is the winner.

Comments

Encourage the pairs to share their results with other pairs. Is there a general pattern? You could change the dice used to show more or fewer numbers and ask the children if they can predict if this will change the results.

Guess the group

This game involves the players in collecting, representing and discussing data, as well as giving opportunities to enhance their knowledge of multiplication and division facts.

Resources

Large space

How to play

Tell the children how many there are in the whole group. Ask them to move around within the space. At a prearranged signal, the children stop and listen for an instruction; e.g. 'Get into groups of 2' ,'Get into groups of 4.' After each grouping, ask the children to check how many people are left over. Is there any size of group that uses all the children?

Change the instructions to include other properties of number; e.g. ask them to create groups with twelve legs, an odd number of heads or a square number of fingers. Encourage the children to think of their own rules to use with the whole group.

Comments

Ask the children to predict how many they think will be left over after each instruction is given. Back in the classroom teams can record the outcomes of the different ways of grouping. Allow discussion between the teams about the recording methods chosen, and what information they show.

Cup drop

This game looks at probability, testing ideas and recording results.

Resources

Plastic cup, tally sheets, pencils and an envelope for each group

How to play

Children work in teams of two or three. The teams agree on a method of dropping the cup and seeing which way it lands. Each drop will fall into one of the following outcomes: standing, upside down or on its side. Each team predicts how many of each outcome will occur in twenty trials. They record their predictions in secret and hand them to you in the envelope provided. Each team member takes a turn at dropping the cup and tallying how it lands. Teams then feed back their results to the whole group. Those whose predictions were the closest in all three categories to the actual results score maximum points.

Comments

Challenge the children to change the way of recording the results. To help create more thoughtful predictions, introduce a sliding scale of scoring: an accurate prediction scores 20 points; for every non-accurate prediction, subtract 2 points. The team with the highest number of points is the winner.

What does it mean?

This game assesses children's knowledge and understanding of different types of graphs, charts and tables.

Resources

Any pre-prepared graph, chart or table

How to play

The children are shown information presented in any way that is appropriate for them. In teams of no more than six, children discuss what the information tells them and the possible causes/reasons for it. Each team is given time to feed back their thoughts. These may be serious, silly or funny as long as they relate directly to what has been shown.

After each team has fed back, as a group they then decide which solution they liked the best and give reasons for their choice. Each team has one vote for their favourite, and no team may vote for themselves. The team with the highest number of votes is the winner. In the case of a tie, voting continues with only the teams that tied scoring.

Comments

This is a good game to play either as formative or summative assessment. Use lists, tables, graphs, diagrams, tally charts, bar charts and line graphs as appropriate.

Record-spinning

This game involves the players in constructing tables to record results.

Resources

Spinners Set A (see page 64), paper clip and pencil per player, paper

How to play

Children are divided into teams of four players named A, B, C and D. Each player has a spinner and a paper clip. Player A has 1, 6 and 9 written in the segments on their spinner; player B has 2, 5 and 11; player C has 3, 8 and 12; and player D has 4, 7 and 10. The paper clip is placed in the centre of the spinner and held in place by a pencil. Each team chooses a method of recording results. Each player flicks the paper clip so that it spins and ends pointing to a number.

The first matches are between players A and B and between C and D, and the winners are the players who spin the highest number. They repeat the game several times and discuss the best way to record the results. The winning players and the losing players then repeat the activity. The overall winner is the player with the greatest number of victories. The results of the game are shared with the whole group. Which method of recording does the group think is the most appropriate and accessible? Why?

Comments

Collect all of the information from all the groups. How would the children present this information? Ask them to design a similar game using different numbers.

Order

This game involves different areas of maths combined with sorting. Any number of children may play.

Resources

Measuring equipment such as a metre rule, scales

How to play

Divide the group into two to four teams. Give every group the same activities to complete: e.g. 'Arrange yourselves in to alphabetical order.' The first group to do this successfully scores a point. Then say 'Arrange yourselves in order of age, youngest first.' Again, the first group to do this successfully scores a point. Continue with instructions such as 'Arrange yourself according to your shoe sizes / heights / birthdays / post codes, and so on.

Comments

Have measuring equipment to hand so that the results can be checked if necessary. Ask the children to think of other criteria for sorting. Be aware of sensitive issues.

Target practice

Children work in small groups in order to test a statement.

Resources

For each team a circular target with internal rings numbered 1–3, three scrunched-up paper balls, recording paper

How to play

Children are divided into teams of 2–4. They test the statement: 'The further you stand from the target, the more accurate the throw will be.' Allow time for them to discuss this. To test their hypothesis, each team member stands one pace from the target and throws the paper ball up to three times at the target; other members record the results, keeping score according to where the paper ball hits the target. When each has had a turn, then move back two paces, repeat, then step back three paces and throw again. A running total is kept. If their results support their hypothesis, they are awarded points.

Comments

As well as the running total, each team should also record the accuracy of the throws as team members moved away from the target. They could invent their own hypothesis to be tested by the group as a whole.

Chance

Play this game after the group has been introduced to the concept of probability.

Resources

Playing cards, coins, 1–6 dice, spinners (see page 64), paper for recording results

How to play

Divide the group into four teams. Each team will play a different game of chance.

Tossing coins: The team members in turn throw a coin and record the number of heads and tails thrown in the set time.

Two dice: The children record their dice throws and how many times they throw a total of 7.

Spinners Set B: Write an equal number of odd and even numbers on the spinners. The children record how often they spin odds and evens.

Cards: The children pick an ace from a single suit of cards displayed face down. Shuffle the cards each time an ace is found.

All children take part. The teams move to the next game after ten minutes. When the time allocated is up, results are collated and discussed as a group.

Comments

Teams could devise their own games of chance for others to play. Extend into a whole-group fair with stalls using their games to test their theories further.

Beetle bug

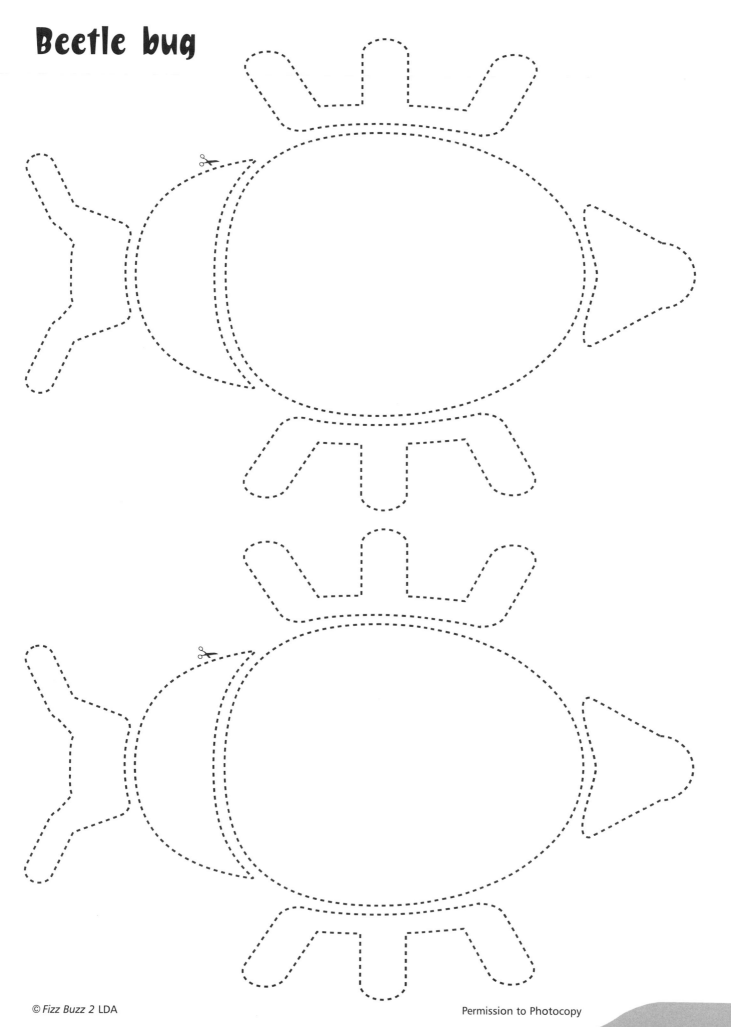

Permission to Photocopy

Spinners

After filling in the blank sections on the spinner, cut each out carefully. The paper clip is placed in the centre of the spinner and held in place by a pencil. Gently flicking the paper clip makes it spin.

Spinners Set A

Spinners Set B